# GUARDIAN ANGELS

"And another angel came, and stood before the altar, having a golden censer; and there was given to him much incense, that he should offer of the prayers of all saints upon the golden altar, which is before the throne of God. And the smoke of the incense of the prayers of the saints ascended up before God from the hand of the angel."

—Apocalypse 8:3-4

"Are they not all ministering spirits, sent to minister for them, who shall receive the inheritance of salvation?"

—Hebrews 1:14

How comforting is the thought that, amid life's dangers and temptations, a celestial spirit is ever at our side to guide and defend us from harm and to lead us safely to our home above!

# THE GUARDIAN ANGELS

## Our Heavenly Companions

*"He hath given his angels charge over thee; to keep thee in all thy ways. In their hands they shall bear thee up: lest thou dash thy foot against a stone."*

—Psalm 90:11-12

TAN BOOKS AND PUBLISHERS, INC.
Rockford, Illinois 61105

Nihil Obstat:     William J. Blacet, J.C.L.
                  Censor Librorum

Imprimatur: ✠ John P. Cody, S.T.D.
                  Apostolic Administrator and Ordinary
                  Diocese of St. Joseph
                  August 29, 1956

Originally published by the Benedictine Convent of Perpetual Adoration, Clyde, Missouri, in 1956 under the title *Our Heavenly Companions*. The type in this book is the property of TAN Books and Publishers, Inc. and, except for brief selections, may not be reproduced without written permission from the Publisher. (This restriction applies only to this *type*, not to quotations from the book.)

ISBN 0-89555-537-9

Library of Congress Catalog Card No. 95-62333

Cover illustration by Heinrich Kaiser (1813-1900).

Printed and bound in the United States of America.


TAN BOOKS AND PUBLISHERS, INC.
P.O. Box 424
Rockford, Illinois 61105
1996

"See that you despise not one of these little ones: for I say to you, that their angels in heaven always see the face of my Father who is in heaven."

– *Matthew* 18:10

St. Francis de Sales (left) and a companion pray to the Guardian Angel of the diocese as they enter the Chablais (France) on a mission to convert the Calvinists back to the Catholic Faith. In four years' time almost the entire population of 72,000 had returned to the Catholic Faith due to St. Francis' preaching and pamphleteering.

# CONTENTS

# From the Catechism
# Of the Council of Trent

"By God's providence Angels have been entrusted with the office of guarding the human race and of accompanying every human being in order to preserve him from any serious dangers . . . our heavenly Father has placed over each of us an Angel under whose protection and vigilance we may be enabled to escape the snares secretly prepared by our enemy, repel the dreadful attacks he makes on us, and under his guiding hand keep to the right road, and thus be secure against all false steps which the wiles of the evil one might cause us to make in order to draw us aside from the path that leads to Heaven." –IV, 9, 4 (p. 502).

Sacred Scripture shows "the benefits bestowed by God on man through the ministry and intervention of Angels, whom He deputes not only on particular and private occasions, but also appoints to take care of us from our very births. He furthermore appoints them to watch over the salvation of each one of the human race." –IV, 9, 5 (p. 503).

# THE
# GUARDIAN ANGELS

*"Behold I will send my angel, who shall go before thee, and keep thee in thy journey, and bring thee into the place that I have prepared . . ."*

—Exodus 23:20-22

## *Chapter 1*

# **Your Best Friend**

D O YOU know who is your best and most faithful friend? It is one whom God Himself has placed at your side as a life companion—a Prince from His own Heavenly Court—your **Guardian Angel.** God in His goodness has appointed him to guide and protect you through life and to lead you safely to your Eternal Home.

From the very beginning of your existence, your Guardian Angel has been concerned about you. He rejoiced when you were born into the world, just as a good mother rejoices over the birth of her child. From the day of your Baptism, you became ever dearer to your Guardian Angel, ever more loved by him. Day and night he watched at your cradle. He led you as you took your first steps. He cared for you with most tender love when danger threatened. He grieved when you committed sin, as if he himself had received the greatest injury, and he left you no peace until you became reconciled with God by a good Confession. He has watched and prayed with you in hours of distress. He has rejoiced with you in days of prosperity. On the day of your First Holy Communion he was the bridal attendant of your soul. As often as you have received the **Bread of Angels** in the state of grace, he has rejoiced to accompany you to the Holy Table. He it was who prayed for you specially when the hand of the bishop anointed you as a soldier of Christ in the Sacrament of Confirmation.

Your Guardian Angel is your best **counselor.** Particularly will he assist young boys and girls in their choice of a **vocation.** He will shield you amid the dangers of the world. If you call upon him, he will help you to find the life companion whom God has destined for you. He will ever remain at your side, so that you may faithfully and conscientiously fulfill the duties of your state in life.

If God has called you to the religious life or to the holy priesthood, your Guardian Angel will protect you from the temptations of the world and help you to preserve your virginal purity, to offer it to God at the altar by your holy vows or to offer the sacred Body of Christ with unstained hands and holy lips as a priest of the Most High.

In short, your Guardian Angel is **your companion in all the circumstances of life**—your friend in good as well as evil days. He will one day assist you in a very special manner—when you enter into **life's last conflict.** Then he will fight with you and for you, until you have won the battle and your heart is at rest. But not even then will he leave you—there where every other, even the best of friends, must leave—on the threshold of eternity. When the light of earth fades away and the brightness of eternity bursts upon you, your Guardian Angel will present your soul before **the tribunal of God** and faithfully **plead your cause.** What is more, if you require purification in the flames of Purgatory, your holy Angel will visit and console you. He will bring before God's throne the good works that are performed for you on earth, and he himself will intercede for you. Finally, when your time of purgation is ended, he will joyfully bring you word of your release from the flames of Purgatory and will lead you to the blissful kingdom of Heaven. But **to benefit** by the presence of this heavenly companion, you must **be docile to his inspirations** and never turn away from this holy Angel who is your guide and your protector.

## Motives for Confidence and Gratitude

What a high value must our souls possess in the sight of our Heavenly Father, that He commissions the princes of His eternal kingdom, His confidants, to protect us, to accompany us every-

where, yes, to bear us up in their hands! What a
new motive for confidence in His love and paternal solicitude! What a powerful incentive for
gratitude to our good Lord and God! If a king of
this world were to send one of his chief courtiers
to a poor subject who was wandering far from his
native country amid many dangers, with the command to guide the poor wanderer to his palace
and protect and shelter him, would such a subject find words to express to his prince the gratitude of his heart? And yet this is but a feeble
representation of the goodness of the King of
Heaven toward us poor children of men who lan-
guish in this valley of tears. Let us therefore render praise, honor and eternal thanksgiving to the
Most High for having given us an Angel as protector and guide to the kingdom of Heaven.

## Scriptural Proofs

Innumerable passages of Holy Scripture
clearly speak of the existence and the protection
of the holy Angels. In the Book of *Exodus* (23:20-
22) God promises to Moses the protection of an
Angel in the wilderness, saying: **"Behold I will
send my angel, who shall go before thee,** and
keep thee in thy journey, and bring thee into the
place that I have prepared. Take notice of him,
and hear his voice, and do not think him one to
be contemned: for he will not forgive when thou

hast sinned, and my name is in him. But if thou wilt hear his voice, and do all that I speak, I will be an enemy to thy enemies, and will afflict them that afflict thee." This beautiful text we may all apply to ourselves, journeying through the wilderness of the world on the way to our heavenly home. But we must also heed the admonition which it contains.

The patriarch **Jacob** commended his grandsons to the protection of his holy Angel: "The Angel that delivereth me from all evils, bless these boys." (Cf. *Gen.* 48:15-16). The book of *Tobias* gives a touching account of the services rendered by the Archangel Raphael to the young Tobias and his solicitude for the young man and his parents. King David frequently mentions the faithful protection of the holy Angels in his Psalms. In beautiful words full of comfort and hope he says of each one of us: "He hath given his angels charge over thee; to keep thee in all thy ways. In their hands they shall bear thee up: lest thou dash thy foot against a stone." (*Ps.* 90:11-12).

Similarly, the Scriptures of the New Testament contain many references to the holy Angels. On one occasion, **Our Lord** Himself said to His disciples: "See that you despise not one of these little ones: for I say to you, that their angels in heaven always see the face of my Father who is in heaven." (*Matt.* 18:10). St. Paul frequently refers to them in his Epistles. When threatened with shipwreck, he encouraged his fellow travelers with the promise that there would be no loss of life among them, saying: "For an angel of God, whose I am, and whom I serve, stood by me this night, saying: Fear not, Paul . . . God hath given thee all them that sail with thee." (*Acts* 27:23-24).

## Teaching of the Fathers

Scriptural references affirming the existence of protecting Angels could be multiplied indefinitely. To those quoted, we add the testimonies of various Fathers of the Church in support of the same teaching:

"Sublime is the dignity of the soul," writes **St. Jerome,** "for to each a Guardian spirit is appointed from the beginning of its existence."

"The Angels have care of us poor pilgrims," writes **St. Augustine;** "they have compassion on us, and at God's command they hasten to our aid, so that we too may once arrive at our common fatherland." Most touchingly he speaks of the constant protection which they extend to us: "The Angels go in and out with us, having their eyes always fixed upon us and upon all that we are doing. If we stop anywhere, they stop also; if we go forth to walk, they bear us company; if we journey into another country, they follow us; go where we will, by land or by sea, they are ever with us . . ."

"My brothers," exhorts **St. Bernard,** "make the holy Angels your friends. Give them joy by having confidential recourse to them, and honor them by your prayers, for they are ever near, to comfort and protect you." Again he writes, "Howsoever weak we may be, howsoever sad our condition, and howsoever great the dangers which surround us, beneath the protection of such guardians we have nothing to fear! Whenever afflictions or temptations frighten you, implore the aid of him who watches over you, who leads you, who succors you in all your necessities."

## Marvelous Goodness of the Angels

Wonderful is the goodness of the Angels in not refusing to bestow their care upon those who commit even venial offenses against their Creator, considering the knowledge they possess of the infinite greatness of the Divine Majesty which is insulted thereby. How amazing, then, to see that they do not abandon **even those wretched persons who live in mortal sin,** who trample underfoot the Blood of the God-man and are guilty of His death! With incredible kindness they continue to watch over these unfortunate souls and spare no effort in bringing them to penance and reconciliation with Almighty God.

But the love of the holy Angels goes further than this: They extend their guardianship also to pagans, to heretics, unbelievers and idolaters, and their protection is not without many good results. It is the opinion of St. Thomas Aquinas that even the Antichrist will have a Guardian Angel, who will restrain him from evil which he would otherwise do. Thus **all men,** howsoever vile and wretched they may be, without a single exception, **are assisted by the holy Angels.** And yet, alas, how little gratitude do these heavenly spirits receive for their tender solicitude! How little love do they receive in return for their boundless love!

## Special Guardians

Every age and condition of life has its **special Guardian Angels.** Infants have their Guardian Angels, who preserve them from danger and guard their innocence. It has often been said that no child would attain to maturity were it not for the protection of his Guardian Angel. This statement finds support in innumerable instances of mysterious protection of little children.

There are Angels charged with the care of **youth,** especially of those exposed to the danger of bad morals. There are Angels animating with zeal, love and devotedness **those engaged in the instruction of youth.** There are Angels of the **clergy,** who inspire them with zeal for preaching the Word of God. There are Angels of **missionaries,** who protect them in danger and encourage them in the hardships of missionary life. There are Angels of the **infidels and pagans,** who constantly intercede for them, that their hearts may open to the light of grace. There are Angels of **those who travel** by air, by land and by water, to protect them from the dangers of collision, fire and explosion, and lead them safely to their destination. There are Guardian Angels of **the sick,** who console them and intercede for them, that they may not lose their merits by impatience. There are Angels who assist **those in the agony of death,** strengthening, encouraging and defending them against the attacks of the infernal enemy.

In the opinion of **St. Clement, St. Gregory the Great, Origen** and other holy writers, **every country, every city, every town and village, and even every family, has a special Guardian Angel.** Believing firmly that every country has its own Guardian Angel, **St. Francis Xavier** invoked the Guardian Angel of every country and city wherein he preached the holy Gospel, and when he left one place to preach elsewhere, he never failed to commend to the protection of the holy Angels the new congregations he had won to the Faith.

Likewise, **altars, churches, parishes, dioceses and religious institutions have their own Guardian Angels.** Every Catholic church has its special Angels to guard it from desecration, and every altar has thousands of Angels to adore the God of Heaven and earth there concealed in the Most Blessed Sacrament.

The holy **Archangel Michael** is honored as the Guardian spirit of the entire Catholic Church, just as he was the Guardian of the chosen people of the Old Testament. It is also believed that he was the special Guardian of Our Lord during His earthly life and that now he is the Guardian of Christ's Vicar on earth, the Holy Father. This holy Archangel revealed to St. Eutropius that he is also the Guardian of the Most Blessed Sacrament.

According to the testimony of the learned historian Baronius, Angels protected the churches of Constantinople and the palace of the Emperor against the attacks of the Arians. The same historian relates that when the Saxons entered a church dedicated to St. Boniface, they were repelled by two Angel warriors, who appeared in wondrous beauty and strength. An Angel protected St. Ambrose and his church when the Empress Justina demanded that he give over to the Arians a basilica in the suburb of Milan.

**Blessed Peter Faber,** a renowned missionary

of the Society of Jesus and the companion of St. Ignatius, its founder, brought many souls to God by his work of evangelization in Germany. While traveling through the diocese of his birth, he received innumerable consolations from the Guardian Angels of several parishes. On repeated occasions he received the most palpable and convincing proofs of their protection. Sometimes these holy Angels preserved him from the fury of the heretics; at other times they rendered souls more mild and tractable to receive from him the doctrine of salvation.

## Visible World Governed by Angels

The protecting love of the holy Angels is carried to such an excess that, not satisfied with thus guarding the souls of men, they even watch over **beasts** and over **the physical world.** According to **St. Augustine,** there are Angels who preside over every visible thing and over all different species of creatures in the world, whether animate or inanimate.

If the all-good God were to open our eyes and show us the Angels under visible forms, what wonders should we discover! Let us consider well and deeply that all the comfort and benefit we derive from earth, air, water, fire—from all creatures—comes to us by the agency of the holy Angels, who are the faithful ministers of God.

## *Chapter 2*

# The Guardian Angels' Services to Us

HOW much we owe to our Guardian Angels! God in His infinite mercy and condescension makes use of their agency to bestow upon the weak and needy children of men an abundance of material and spiritual blessings. The Angels are the first-born "children" of the Heavenly Father and as such are our elder "brothers," forming with us but one great family of God. Just as parents sometimes entrust the younger members of the family to the care of their elder brothers and sisters, so **our Heavenly Father** commits us to the care of the holy Angels. But the love of the Angels for their charges upon earth far exceeds in strength and tenderness the love of a brother or sister, or even that of parents.

If we but knew all the favors which we continually receive from the holy Angels, our hearts would indeed be harder than stone not to be sensibly affected thereby. It would be necessary to

reckon up all the evils which can befall us—
whether in mind or body, in our spiritual or temporal goods, in regard to our private or public
interests, by wars, pestilences or famines—in
order to specify all the various kinds of assistance
we receive from the Angels. Their constant
thought and unremitting care is to **preserve us
from sin,** or to deliver us from it when we have
fallen. They obtain powerful graces for us from
the mercy of God, moderate our passions,
remove hindrances to our use of grace and assist
us to triumph over the evil one in temptations.
They discover to us our faults and imperfections
and move us to sincere contrition.

**Father Faber** touchingly describes this solicitude of our Guardian Angels: "Ever at our side is
being lived a golden life. A princely Spirit is
there who sees God and enjoys the bewildering
splendors of His Face, even there where he is,
nearer than the limits of our outstretched arms.
An unseen warfare is waging round our steps,
but that beautiful Spirit lets not so much as the
sound of it vex our ears. He fights for us and asks
no thanks, but hides his silent victories, and con-
tinues to gaze upon God. His tenderness for us is
above all words. His office will last beyond the
grave, until at length it merges into a still sweeter
tie of something like heavenly equality, when on
the morning of the resurrection we pledge each
other, in those first moments, to an endless

blessed love. Till then we shall never know from how many dangers he has delivered us, nor how much of our salvation is actually due to him. Meanwhile he merits nothing by the solicitudes of his office. He is beyond the power of meriting, for he has attained the sight of God. His work is a **work of love** because his sweet presence at our side he knows to be a part of God's eternal creative love towards our particular soul."

"Wherever we go," writes **Cardinal O'Connell** in his beautiful pastoral on the holy Angels, "this Angelic partnership is never interrupted. Heavenly Spirits shield us from bodily danger and minister to us in our temporal needs . . . Intent upon **the salvation of our souls,** they instruct us, they protect us, they plead for us with God. They ward off temptations, overcome obstacles—physical as well as spiritual—and pointing out the path of virtue, they guide us lest we go astray. To our prayers they unite theirs; they inspire holy thoughts or whisper helpful inspirations: at times, too, they inflict upon us healing and salutary chastisements. To every want of the soul through life they minister, that they may assist it to arrive safely at its journey's end. All this they do for us, if we but let them; every help that they can give us is ours, if we but welcome them and gratefully co-operate with them.

"Many are the motives which prompt such **constant devotion to our interests.** These celestial patrons, we know, are close to the merciful Heart of the Redeemer; they understand, therefore, His untiring concern for our welfare, and from that inexhaustible Fountain of love they imbibe the tenderest affection in our regard. They know, too, that we, their relatives—not by the flesh but through the spirit element in our nature—are destined to share their glory, to be their fellow-citizens in Heaven, and one day to enter into their unending companionship. In the unselfishness of their love, they are anxious for the period of our probation to close triumphantly.

"However, what especially enhances the intensity of their affection is the fact that they have a **Divine commission to watch over us** and to be for us here upon earth the instruments of God's mercies. This it is that urges them to sweep down from their golden skies, to flash swiftly and joyously through the dim air of this lower world, that they may assure us of their love and be at hand in all fear and trouble.

"And with what admirable solicitude and unceasing watchfulness do these protecting Angels fulfill their Divine commission with regard to us! **At every moment, though unseen, they are by our side.** They never forsake us from the first breath we draw until we have entered into the possession of our eternal destiny. They hover about **the babe** slumbering in its crib; they guide the timid and untried steps with which **childhood** and **youth** enter upon life, at first so strange and at all times so full of peril. They hold out a helping hand to strong and rugged **manhood,** seasoned by struggles with the forces of evil, and bearing, perhaps, the scars which the wounds of sins have made. And when the light of life is transformed into the darkness and gloom of **age,** with its dreams unrealized and its hopes cherished in vain, Guardian Angels are near to support the bent form and tottering steps, and to banish the shadows of loneliness and sorrow."

The good offices which the holy Guardian Angels perform in our behalf may be briefly summed up as follows:

1. They preserve us from many unknown dangers to soul and body.

2. They defend us against the temptations of the evil spirits.

3. They inspire us with holy thoughts and prompt us to deeds of virtue in the Divine service.

4. They warn us of spiritual dangers and admonish us when we have sinned.

5. They unite with us in prayer and offer our prayers to God.

6. They defend us at the hour of death against the last attacks of our spiritual foes.

7. They console the souls languishing in Purgatory and conduct them to Heaven when their faults have been fully expiated.

# 1. They Protect Us in Perils

Innumerable instances of the protection of the Angels in **physical dangers** may be cited from Holy Scripture, from the lives of the Saints and from the daily experience of ordinary persons. Among those mentioned in the Scriptures are the rescue of **Lot** and his family from the city of Sodom, the protection of the **three Hebrew youths** in the fiery furnace of Babylon, the assistance rendered to **Judas the Machabee** and his army, and the rescue of **St. Peter** in prison.

In the life of **St. Gregory of Tours** it is related that while he was still a boy his father became dangerously ill. The devoted son prayed earnestly for his good father. That night his Guardian Angel appeared to him in sleep, saying: "Arise, write the Name of Jesus on a small wooden chip and lay it on your father's pillow." In the morning Gregory related the vision to his mother, who bade him do as he had been told. He obeyed, and the father immediately regained his health. Two years later, the father again became ill. Gregory once more had recourse to prayer, and again his Guardian Angel appeared to him in sleep, instructing him to use the liver of a fish, as had been done in the case of Tobias. This admonition was followed and the father was cured a second time.

A striking incident of recent occurrence in one of our Southern states was the rescue of a young boy from drowning. On a bright, sunny day in May, Sister M. took her pupils to the woods to pick berries. After the merry group had spent a happy day and had filled all their baskets with berries, they started for home. On their homeward journey, it was necessary to cross a small stream, and several of the older boys asked permission to wade across rather than to cross on the bridge. As the stream had every appearance of being shallow, Sister M. readily granted the permission.

One of the most sturdy boys went ahead, but what was the surprise and horror of all when he suddenly disappeared from sight beneath the water! He had stepped into a deep hole, and as he was unable to swim, he floundered helplessly about, unable to regain his footing. Sister M. ordered all the other boys back to the bank of the stream, and with a fervent invocation to her Guardian Angel—whose help she had often experienced—she herself was preparing to go to the rescue of the boy, who had just gone down for the second time.

Suddenly, as if by magic, **two stalwart youths** stepped out of an automobile, which had come up unnoticed, and went hurriedly to the bank. One of them stood beside Sister, while the other, without a word, descended into the water up to his head, took the boy in his arms and carried him safely back to his teacher.

Sister thanked the young man most cordially and inquired his name. He merely smiled and said: "What does it matter—the boy is safe." Astonishing to relate, his clothes seemed perfectly dry when he and his companion returned to the car. Then they left so quickly that no trace could be seen of them on the road. Sister M. breathed a prayer of thanksgiving to her good Guardian Angel, for she was firmly convinced that it was he who had once again come to her assistance.

Though the holy Angels are most solicitous for our bodily welfare, yet still greater is their solicitude for the welfare of **immortal souls.** It is especially when the virtue of **holy purity** is assailed that the Guardian Angels lend their powerful protection to their proteges, as is witnessed in the lives of St. Agnes, St. Agatha, St. Cecilia, St. Lucy, St. Theophila and other Saints.

A touching story of a Guardian Angel's protection of an innocent youth is related by the renowned Jesuit, Father Coret. One day in 1638, **a young nobleman** appeared at the monastery at noon and asked to see a certain priest. The priest came and, immediately upon seeing the stranger, received the impression that this was an Angel. The heavenly appearance, the majestic bearing and the angelic demeanor of the young man were most striking. His countenance was fair, his eyes exceedingly kind, his hair blond, his features mild and delicate. The noble visitor apologized for coming at so inconvenient a time, but added, "The zeal with which you labor for the honor of God and the salvation of youth urges me to leave nothing undone when the innocence and perhaps the eternal salvation of one of your pupils is in peril. You are acquainted with the youth, *N.*?" The young man in question was a nobleman, about sixteen years of age, very handsome, possessed of great virtue and beloved by all. "Oh, how you would love him if you knew him as I do!" continued the stranger. "He is an angel, but alas, into what danger of temptation will he be led today! He has been invited to a banquet. If he goes, it will be at the price of his innocence; he will suffer an irreparable loss!"

Naturally, the priest was greatly surprised at this statement. He inquired of the stranger who he was and how he had learned of the snares which had been laid for the youth, but he received no other answer than that the youth was as pure as an angel, very dear to God, and that his Guardian Angel was most solicitous to preserve his innocence. Then the stranger added, "Often I am in the midst of those who would lead him astray. I come in the name of God and conjure you to prevent so great an evil. Be convinced that **as the demons exert all their power to corrupt youth, the Guardian Angels likewise do their utmost to protect them.**"

The stranger took his leave, and the priest hastened to inform the mother and the son of what had happened. He then made a search for his distinguished visitor, but he was never seen again, and the priest never doubted that this had been the youth's Guardian Angel.

## 2. They Defend Us against the Demons

In the hour of **temptation,** when the enemies from Hell break in upon us, the holy Angels **intervene** in our behalf and **help us to conquer** the craftiness of the enemy. They **strengthen** us in the fight, **warn** us against the suggestions of the tempter, **disclose** to us his snares and **make us fear evil**. The fallen angels, retaining the keen and penetrating knowledge proper to their spirit nature, wage fierce and constant battles against those creatures whom God had commanded them to serve. In their morbid despair and jealousy, with a strength surpassing the utmost might of man, they aim at our destruction. "Our wrestling," says **St. Paul,** "is not against flesh and blood, but against the principalities and the powers, against the rulers of the world of this darkness, against the spirits of wickedness in the high places." (*Eph.* 6:12). But the paternal care of God shields us from their malevolent attacks by surrounding us with the protection of our good Angels. "God," says **St. Augustine,** "has subjected the bad angels to the good; they cannot do as much harm as they wish, but only as much as they are permitted for our trial and punishment."

**St. Meinrad,** a fervent son of St. Benedict, withdrew into the solitude of the mountains to devote himself to the contemplative life. Here he was often besieged by evil spirits, who sought to overthrow his virtue. But the Saint had recourse to his Guardian Angel, and each time he was assaulted, it seemed to him as if his holy Angel stood at his side, lovingly encouraging him and assisting him in the conflict.

To **St. Margaret of Cortona** an evil spirit one day appeared, seeking to terrify her. But at the same moment her Guardian Angel also appeared and said, "Fear not, daughter, and do not lose courage. The demon is less powerful to harm you than one who is trodden underfoot by his conqueror. I am with you—I, the Guardian Angel of your soul, which is an exalted abode of God."

## 3. They Inspire Holy Thoughts

"Your holy Angel is tender, gentle and mild," says the devout spiritual writer, Hermas. "When he takes possession of your heart, he speaks of justice, modesty and benignity, of true love and piety.

When such things make themselves felt in your heart, know that your holy Angel is with you."

It is peculiar to the good Angels to enlighten and instruct the soul of man, to inspire it with strength and fortitude and also, by spiritual consolations, by gentle persuasions, by calmness and refreshing peace, to lighten the fulfillment of every duty and to remove all hindrances to advancement in virtue. "Return to thy mistress, and humble thyself under her hand" (*Gen.* 16:9), said an Angel to **Agar,** the handmaid of Abraham and Sara, thus reminding her of her duty. **St. Raphael** taught the young **Tobias** how he should enter the married state in the holy fear of God and how, together with his parents, he should adore and praise God. (Cf. *Tob.* 11-12). Likewise, it was an Angel who exhorted the Roman centurion **Cornelius** to seek out St. Peter in order to be instructed by him in the True Faith. (Cf. *Acts* 10:30).

## 4. They Warn and Admonish Us

Before the city of Jerusalem was captured by the Romans, voices were heard above the Temple saying, "Let us withdraw from hence!" Similarly, our holy Guardian Angel often urges us to leave those places, those companionships, those conversations, books and pastimes where danger threatens our soul and where, because of his angelic purity and delicacy, he cannot bear us company. His voice cries out to us in various ways—through the counsel of a **friend**, through the reading of a good **book**, through the voice of **conscience**, etc. How often, how lovingly, how mildly he instructs, warns, entreats and invites us! He is most anxious to be our **advocate** at the throne of God, but if we do not heed his voice he will be compelled to be our **accuser,** for he can only fulfill his sublime task if we cooperate with him with ready willingness. If we harden our heart and refuse to heed his admonitions, he will one day be compelled to reveal our sins before all the world. Disobedience on our part would therefore be not only the basest ingratitude, but the greatest folly as well, for it is only for our own eternal welfare that our Angel thus warns us.

Our Guardian Angel is likewise our loving **admonitor.** To reprove is an act very proper to love, for since love cherishes an inmost desire for the good of the beloved and shows itself also in deed, so it seeks to avert evil from the one beloved. The administering of reproofs is a means toward this end, and this the Angel accomplishes by inflicting the sting of **remorse of conscience**. The moment we have committed sin, our holy Angel withdraws his consolations and pierces our soul with pain. He strives to awaken in our heart vehement qualms of conscience and to move us to **true contrition** and **penance.** How great are our obligations toward this **true friend** who thus warns us of evil, chastises us and fills us with anxiety when we have done wrong!

## 5. They Pray with Us and for Us

Holy Scripture clearly teaches that the Angels pray in our behalf. The Prophet **Zacharias,** speaking of the supplicating Angels who were watching over Jerusalem, says, "The angel of the Lord answered, and said: 'O Lord of hosts, how long wilt thou not have mercy on Jerusalem, and the cities of Juda?'" (*Zach.* 1:12). And the **Archangel Raphael** said to Tobias, "When thou didst pray with tears . . . I offered thy prayer to the Lord." (*Tob.* 12:12). **St. Augustine** says: "The Angels pray for us, not as if God did not know our needs, but the sooner to obtain for us the gift of His mercy and to secure for us the blessings of His grace."

On one occasion, while assisting at Holy Mass with special fervor, **St. Gertrude** was rapt in ecstasy. In this state she saw her Guardian Angel bearing her prayers to the throne of the Divine Majesty, presenting them to the three Divine Persons and imploring them to hear her petitions. The prayer of the Guardian Angel was accepted and Gertrude was blessed by each Person of the Godhead.

**St. Bernard** frequently admonished his disciples to conduct themselves in an edifying manner in the performance of their devotional exercises, lest their Guardian Angels, who took part in them, should withdraw. "How happy you would be," he exclaimed, "if you could see how they hasten to join those who sing the Psalms and with what reverential bearing they remain among them! They assist those who pray and meditate. With great solicitude they go back and forth between God and us, bearing our sighs to the throne of God. Let us therefore strive earnestly to make their joy complete."

It is related that **St. Gregory of Tours** and others who slept at the time of prayer received a blow from their Guardian Angel. The histories of religious orders recount many instances of holy souls being awakened by their Angels for prayer in the morning and being punished by them for small faults, such as not rising immediately or not giving themselves to meditation with sufficient fervor.

## 6. They Assist Us at the Hour of Death

Especially at the **hour of death**, when the wicked enemies redouble their assaults in order to win the **decisive battle for eternity,** our Guardian Angel will assist us if we have been faithful to him during life. We read in the lives of many Saints that their Guardian Angels were visibly present at their last hour, comforting them in their final struggle, strengthening them against the redoubled attacks of Hell, announcing to them the hour of their death and giving them the assurance that they would be heirs of the kingdom of Heaven. Not a few of the Saints at their death were seen being carried by exultant Angels into the heavenly Paradise. Frequently, too, the holy Guardian Angels have procured for their proteges the grace of a happy death by calling a priest to administer the Last Sacraments.

In the acts of **St. John of Avila** of Spain, we find the following incident, the Saint himself vouching for its truth:

In the year 1585, the Rev. Father Centenares, a member of St. John's community, was awakened one stormy night and requested to take **Holy Viaticum** to a dying person. At first the priest hesitated and thought to wait until morning, as he did not know the way and the night was very dark. But the love of God triumphed over fear, and he started out, taking with him two consecrated Hosts. But scarcely had he left the church when **two youths** of heavenly appearance placed themselves at his right and left side. They held burning candles, which were not extinguished by the falling rain, and accompanied the priest to the sick person and back again to the church.

When he had placed the Sacred Host in the tabernacle, they vanished as suddenly as they had appeared. While the good priest was wondering in astonishment at this occurrence, he received a message from St. John which contained the words: "Do not be astonished at what has happened to you this night. It is quite certain that the two youths whom you saw were Angels sent by God to reward your zeal . . ."

## 7. They Console the Poor Souls

One of the most beautiful and consoling features of the Church's teaching concerning the Guardian Angels is the fact that the **mission** of the holy Angels **does not terminate with the earthly life** of their charges, but only upon the entrance into Paradise of those souls committed to their care. Should it happen that at the moment of death a soul in the state of grace is not yet worthy to behold the face of the Most High, the Angel Guardian conducts it to **Purgatory**—the place of its purification and expiation—and thereafter is most zealous in procuring for it all the assistance and consolation in his power.

A touching incident is related in the chronicles of the Jesuit Order concerning the zeal of the holy Angels in gathering suffrages for the souls in Purgatory. A holy priest of that order was in the habit of reciting the Rosary every day for the Poor Souls in Purgatory. One day, through inadvertence, he retired without having recited it, but scarcely had he fallen asleep when he was awakened by his Guardian Angel, who said, "My son, the souls in Purgatory are awaiting the usual performance of your charity."

In the writings of the holy Fathers it is revealed that the celestial messengers of mercy go even further. They descend to the altars of earth, and drawing the **Precious Blood** of Jesus Christ from the golden chalices during the thousands of Holy Masses daily celebrated, they shower it like a cool dew upon Purgatory.

**St. Margaret Mary Alacoque** was one day transported in spirit into Purgatory. There she beheld, among other things, an immense space filled with flames and glowing coals and, amid these, a great number of Poor Souls in human form, raising their hands to Heaven and imploring mercy. But all the while their Guardian Angels were at their side, inspiring them with courage and comforting them in the most tender manner.

The Guardian Angels assist with a special zeal those souls in Purgatory who have been most devoted to them during life.

It is the teaching of some spiritual writers that the Angels inform the suffering souls of the happenings in this world about which those souls would be concerned. **St. Augustine** tells us that "the departed may be informed by the Angels of things happening in the world, insofar as this is permitted by Him to whose judgment everything is subject." It is likewise believed that the Angels reveal to the Poor Souls the benefactors who are assisting them by their prayers, and at the same time urge the suffering souls to pray for these good friends.

As soon as the **hour of release** has struck for one of the suffering souls, the Guardian Angel of that happy soul is commissioned by God to descend into Purgatory, to open the doors of its prison and to lead the delivered soul without delay into the eternal habitations of Paradise. The good Angel descends with the rapidity of lightning into the dismal prison of pain to carry out the work of release because his love for his cherished ward urges him to liberate the Poor Soul and to lead it to the sight and possession of God. The Guardian Angel is often accompanied by other Angels or by a whole multitude of Angels, and then the entrance of the released soul is truly a triumphant one.

Though the assistance which the holy Angels render to the souls in Purgatory is very consoling, yet it is to be feared that some persons consigned to the purging flames may be deprived of the aid of the Angels because during life they were not devoted to their Guardian Angel or because they neglected to aid the Poor Souls.

## Chapter 3

# Our Duties toward Our Guardian Angels

REAT indeed is our **debt of gratitude** to our Guardian Angel for his tender and untiring solicitude in our behalf. Not until we enter eternity shall we know the number of benefits which have come to us through his agency from the first moment of our existence. With **Tobias,** we ought therefore to exclaim in deepest gratitude: "What wages shall we give him, or what can be worthy of his benefits?" (*Tob.* 12:2).

**St. Bernard** tells us that we owe our Guardian Angel profound **respect** for his presence, **confidence** in his love and power to protect us, and **gratitude** for the great benefits which he confers upon us. "Always remember that you are in the presence of your Guardian Angel," he exhorts his disciples. "In whatever place you may be, in whatever secret recess you may hide, think of your Guardian Angel. Never do in the presence of your Angel what you would not do in my presence."

The great dignity and sanctity of the holy Angels makes the duty of **reverence** an indispensable one for us. Before the great ones of earth, men are very modest and respectful, yet the dignity of earthly kings and princes is incomparably less than that of the lowest of the Angels. Therefore, we should always conduct ourselves piously and modestly before our holy Angel, refraining from every word, gesture or action which could displease or grieve our heavenly friend and guide. This continual remembrance of the presence of our holy Angel is also an excellent means of overcoming temptation.

If we truly love our Guardian Angel, we cannot fail to have a **boundless confidence** in his powerful intercession with God and a firm faith in his willingness to help us. This will inspire us frequently to **invoke his aid** and protection, especially in time of temptation. It will prompt us also to **ask his counsel** in the many problems which confront us, in matters both great and small. Many of the Saints made it a practice never to undertake anything without first seeking advice of their Guardian Angel. The words which God addressed to the people of Israel, our Guardian Angel also addresses to us: "Call upon me in all necessities, in all dangers and temptations; I will protect and assist you, and your prayer will contribute to my glory."

Above all, we owe to our faithful Guardian Angel the most **profound gratitude** for the numberless benefits he bestows upon us. Like the young Tobias, we too are overwhelmed with **continual benefits** by our good Angel. Always and everywhere he stands at our side, lovingly protecting us, kindly warning us and earnestly exhorting us. In no way can we better prove our gratitude than by obediently following his admonitions and showing a tender filial devotion toward him.

## Devotion to Our Angel Guardian

In recognition of his loving service, we ought to practice tender devotion to our Guardian Angel and live in loving familiarity with him. **Every day of our life** should be a day of devotion to him and of thanksgiving for his marvelous goodness to us.

The **following suggestions** may assist in the practice of this devotion: **Upon awakening** in the morning, greet this devoted prince of Heaven who kept faithful watch at your side while you slept; thank him and ask him to accompany and protect you throughout the day. **While dressing,** show reverence for his presence by your modesty. **At the commencement of prayer,** beg him to enlighten, counsel and protect you, so that at the close of the day he may with joy offer your labors to God.

**When leaving the house,** and particularly when going on a journey, offer him a friendly invitation to accompany you. **When the clock strikes,** utter an ejaculation such as, "My dear Guardian Angel, assist me at the hour of my death," or "O blessed Angel, I love you and I wish to love you more and more." And **at night,** thank him for his protection and for the many services he has rendered so willingly. In this way, each day may be spent in loving companionship with your dear Angel, and you may confidently rely upon his assistance in every circumstance, particularly at the hour of death.

Another practice which will be pleasing to our Guardian Angel is to choose one day of the week to honor him in a particular way by offering special prayers, assisting at Holy Mass and receiving Holy Communion in his honor, etc. **Tuesday,** which is dedicated to the holy Angels, may be fittingly chosen for this purpose. Especially on our birthday and on the anniversary of our Baptism ought we to honor our Guardian Angel. Some persons have a beautiful custom of giving as large a sum in alms as they have lived years, or of offering as many acts of virtue or acts of devotion. On these days especially we ought to thank our holy Angel for the many favors he has granted us and to implore him to exercise his holy office of guardianship until death and not permit us to depart out of this life without receiving the Last Sacraments.

Our late Holy Father, **Pope Pius XI,** in an audience granted to a group of children, urged them to practice fervent devotion to their Guardian Angels, invoking them at the beginning and at the end of each day and often during the day. "In this," the Holy Father said, "you can imitate what the Pope really does. At the beginning of each day of his life, and every evening at the end of the day, he invokes his Guardian Angel; and he often repeats these invocations during the course of the day, especially when things become a little complicated and difficult, which often happens. And We wish to say, also, as a debt of gratitude to Our Guardian Angel, that **We have always felt Ourselves assisted by him in some admirable way.** Often We feel and perceive that Our Angel is near Us, ready to help Us, to assist Us. And this each Guardian Angel does equally for each one of you."

The devout spiritual writer Boudon, whose inspiring book, *Devotion to the Nine Choirs of Angels,* we have frequently consulted in the preparation of this little work, gives the following suggestion for venerating our Guardian Angel: "Choose, therefore, sometimes a quarter of an hour, half an hour, an hour or more and, retiring apart, **converse at leisure with your good Angel.** Place yourself on your knees before him, prostrate yourself on the ground—for it is well to adopt this practice occasionally when alone; ask his pardon for your ingratitude; beg his holy benediction; say all that a good heart would prompt one to say to a faithful and loving friend. Speak to him at one time of your needs, of your miserable failings, of your temptations, of your weaknesses; at another of Divine love—and of the holy ways which lead to God. Converse with him sometimes concerning the offenses which men commit against their Sovereign Lord Jesus and His most blessed Mother; at other times, consider in detail the obligations you are under to him, his goodness to you, his beauty, his perfections, his admirable qualities. Deal with him as with a kind father, as with a loving mother, a true brother, an incomparable friend, a zealous lover, a vigilant pastor, a charitable guide, the witness of your most important secrets, a learned physician to heal all your ailments, an advocate, a powerful protector and a compassionate judge; invoke him in all these characters, and in others which your love will suggest to you. They will serve you as so many considerations which will make you pass your time much more agreeably than with the creatures of earth."

## Venerating the Guardians of Others

Besides practicing a tender devotion to our own Guardian Angel, we ought also to adopt the laudable practice of venerating the Guardian Angels of others. When we meet persons of our acquaintance, we should, at the same time that we greet them, also lovingly salute their Guardian Angel. This can be done by an interior act, without attracting notice. Or, we may make the good intention and renew it from time to time, that as often as we salute anyone, we purpose at the same time to salute his holy Angel. Soon it will become very easy for us to remember these holy Angels, and we will receive many blessings from them.

Let us frequently venerate **the Guardian Angel of our Patron Saint** and thank him for having done so much for the sanctification of his or her soul. We ought also to honor **the Guardian Angels of our parents,** our **sisters** and **brothers,** of our **relatives** and **friends,** whose Angels often render us services which we would not receive from our own Angel, perhaps because of some advantage to the souls of our dear ones from the good we do them.

Particular respect ought also to be paid to the Princes of Heaven who guard the **Sovereign Pontiff,** the **Bishops,** especially the Bishop of the diocese in which we reside, and other persons who preside over the Church. Let us ask **the Angel Guardians of the ecclesiastics** to assist them, that they may succeed in establishing the reign of Jesus Christ in the hearts of the faithful entrusted to their care, that they may destroy the empire of Satan and receive the light and strength necessary to maintain holy discipline in their respective jurisdictions. Let us also frequently honor **the Guardian Angels of our confessors** and **spiritual**

**directors,** beseeching these good Angels to inspire them with such counsels as are purely conformable to the Divine will.

**The Guardian Angels of the country,** the **state,** the **city** or **town,** the **diocese** and the **parish** in which we live are likewise deserving of our loving and grateful veneration. We ought often and earnestly to recommend to these holy Angels the places entrusted to their guardianship and, while we thank them for past protection, also implore them to arrest by their prayers the torrent of vice and immorality which so loudly demands vengeance and to avert the wrath of the Most High, provoked by the many offenses committed against Him.

In addition, let us honor **the Guardian Angels of heathens, heretics** and **infidels,** and from time to time go in spirit to converse with them and to express the regret of our hearts at the unbelief of those over whom they have charge. For alas, far from thanking the Angels for their loving care, these poor infidels do not even know that they are assisted by them!

When we enter a church or any other place where numbers of persons are assembled, let us not fail to **salute all the Guardian Angels present.** When we walk through the crowded streets of a city or town, let us contemplate interiorly the Angels who accompany all this multitude. When we are on a journey, let us remember that all the towns or cities we pass through contain as many Guardian Angels as there are inhabitants, and let us send them a loving salutation from our heart. These heavenly Princes will favorably regard the honor we show them and will be constrained to make us some return, for the Angels are incomparable in their gratitude.

When keeping the festival of a Saint, it is a commendable practice to form the intention of honoring at the same time the holy Angel who was his guardian here below. We need not multiply our devotions on this account, but only make the intention of honoring the holy Angel by all the good works we perform in the Saint's honor. By this means we may keep the feasts of many different Angels during the year. Thus we will gain the favor of all these heavenly spirits and will draw down upon ourselves the sweetest benedictions of Paradise.

If we thus cultivate the friendship of the Angels, we shall indeed be blessed, for no earthly friends can vie with them in goodness, in power and in love. **St. Denis**, who wrote most inspiringly of the holy Angels, delighted in assuming the title of "Philangelus," that is, "Friend of the Angels."

Let us take to heart the advice of **Pope St. Leo the Great**: "Make friendships with the holy Angels," and we shall find in them most loving **companions** in our earthly exile, our **champions** against the malice and rage of the devils, our **advocates** at the judgment seat of God and our amiable **companions in bliss and glory** throughout the endless years of eternity.

## *Chapter 4*

# The "Bread of Angels"

Fittingly is **the Blessed Sacrament** called the **"Bread of Angels,"** because of the ardent **love** with which the Angels cherish the adorable Sacrament and the profound **adoration** which they render to their God hidden beneath the sacramental veils. But this designation reminds us also of the **angelic purity** which ought to adorn **our hearts when we receive Holy Communion.** We ought, therefore, to think of our Guardian Angels and their incomparable purity whenever we approach the Table of the Lord, asking them to obtain for us the grace to approach the Heavenly Banquet with true purity of heart and worthy dispositions.

It is particularly **when we approach the Holy Table** that our Guardian Angels exercise their most watchful care over us, for here there is question of a very special homage to their most beloved Lord in the wondrous condescension of His Eucharistic state. With what glowing love they hasten to render Him their services! And yet the Holy Eucharist was instituted **not for the Angels, but for men**. Ought we not to be wholly abashed in contemplating the Angels' fervor?

When we are preparing for Holy Communion, the Angels strive to awaken in us **holy sentiments;** they urge us to **banish distractions** and to repeat pious **acts of contrition, longing** and **love.** The evil spirit takes delight in disturbing us in order to hinder us from receiving Holy Communion fruitfully, for he knows that this is the fountain of all good. On this account, we often experience that just during Holy Mass and at the time of Holy Communion we are most violently assailed by distractions and temptations. But our faithful Angel also redoubles his watchfulness at this sacred time, and if we cooperate with him, he will assist us to conquer the enemy and to receive the adorable Sacrament with proper dispositions. We must also strive not to displease our good Angel by want of reverence in approaching the Holy Table.

Our holy Guardian Angels also rejoice in uniting with us in **adoration** before the Most Blessed Sacrament and during the time of Holy Mass. They do all they can to keep us from inattention and irreverence, for they are inflamed with love of God, whom they behold face to face.

**St. Francis de Sales** had special devotion toward the holy Angels charged with the guardianship of the tabernacles. His veneration for these Angelic Guardians was increased by an instance which showed that these pure spirits revere not only the Sacred Species, but also the ministers who consecrate and handle them. After having conferred Holy Orders on a pious young man, St. Francis noticed that the newly ordained priest hesitated before a door as if to let someone pass before him. "Why do you pause?" asked the Saint. "God favors me with the sight of my Guardian Angel," replied the priest. "Before I was ordained to the holy priesthood, my Angel always remained at my right and preceded me. Now he walks at the left and refuses to go before me." Such is the great veneration which the Angelic spirits show even to God's ministers because of their reverence for the Blessed Sacrament.

It is related of **St. Catherine of Siena**, who was also favored with the visible presence of her Guardian Angel, that once while praying in the church she turned her head slightly to gratify her curiosity. Her Guardian Angel gave her so severe a look for her disrespect in the presence of the Most Holy that for several days St. Catherine was inconsolable and performed severe penance in atonement.

**Blessed Veronica of Binasco** relates a similar experience: "Once," she writes, "when, prompted by curiosity, I happened during the time of Mass to look at one of the Sisters who was kneeling near the altar, the Angel of God who is constantly beside me rebuked me with such severity that I almost fainted with terror. How threateningly he looked at me as he said, 'Why dost thou not keep watch over thy heart? Why dost thou gaze thus curiously at thy sister? Thou hast committed no slight offense against God.' Thus spoke the Angel, and by Christ's command he enjoined on me a heavy penance for my fault, which for three days I bewailed with tears. Now, when I hear Mass, I never venture so much as to turn my head, for fear of incurring the displeasure of the Divine Majesty." What a lesson for those who give free rein to their eyes in church and even talk during the time of Holy Mass!

## Chapter 5

# The Saints and Their Guardian Angels

HE lives of nearly all the Saints reveal that they had special devotion to their Guardian Angels. Many of them were privileged with the familiar companionship of their Angels and received visible proofs of the services which the holy Angels render to those under their charge.

**St. Rose of Lima**, the first American blossom of sanctity upon whom Holy Church conferred public veneration, lived a life of great purity and innocence. From early childhood she was privileged to hold familiar conversations with the holy Angels. She was delivered by her holy Angel from numerous difficulties and dangers, and she once declared that her Guardian Angel did whatever she asked him to do.

**St. Gemma Galgani** likewise cherished a tender devotion to her Guardian Angel and often employed him as a messenger to deliver her letters.

**Pope St. Gregory the Great** was tenderly devoted to his Guardian Angel. It was to his Guardian Angel that he owed the obtaining of the papal dignity. During the time the Saint was abbot of a monastery he had built in Rome, his Guardian Angel frequently appeared to him disguised as a poor merchant and begged for an alms. After he became Pope, St. Gregory adopted the custom of daily feeding twelve poor persons. Among these he beheld one whose virtuous bearing impressed him deeply. Upon inquiring of this person who he was, he received the reply, "I am the poor merchant to whom you gave, besides twelve dollars, the silver dish of your mother. This act of charity which I caused you to perform prepared you for the dignity of high priest. I am your Angel. Fear not, Gregory. God sent me to tell you that you would obtain everything you asked for through my service. As I was the cause of your being raised to the Chair of St. Peter, I shall also protect and preserve you in this position until death."

We read in the life of **St. Frances of Rome** that during the latter half of her life she enjoyed the singular grace of seeing her Guardian Angel ever at her side. She thus describes this heavenly companion: "His aspect is full of sweetness and majesty. His eyes are generally turned toward

Heaven, and words cannot describe the Divine purity of that gaze. His brow is always serene; his glances kindle in the soul the flames of ardent devotion. When I look upon him, I understand the glory of the angelic nature and the degraded condition of our own." Her wish had always been to attain a perfect conformity with the Divine will, and now this mysterious guidance furnished her with the means of knowing that will in its minutest details. In her struggles with the evil one, the Angel became her shield of defense.

The presence of her heavenly Guide was also to Frances a mirror in which she could see reflected all her imperfections. When she committed **the slightest fault**, the Angel disappeared; and it was only after she had carefully examined her conscience, discovered her failing, lamented and humbly confessed it, that he returned. On the other hand, when she was only disturbed by a **doubt** or a **scruple**, he dissipated her uneasiness by a look of great kindness. His guidance enlightened her chiefly with regard to the difficulty she had in submitting to certain cares and obligations which belonged to her position as mistress of a family. She was wont to imagine that the hours thus employed were lost in God's sight, but the celestial Guardian corrected her judgment on this point and taught her to discern the Divine will in every little irksome duty, in every contradiction, great or small, as well as in great trials and on important occasions.

**St. Margaret of Cortona** was, by the grace of God, converted from a great sinner into a fervent penitent. One day, as she was earnestly praying for the conversion of sinners, our Saviour revealed to her that **His Heart** desires nothing so much as **the conversion of sinners** and that He is always ready to forgive. He said, "I even send My Angels to assist them and urge them by repeated inspirations to abandon the ways of sin." Margaret then asked Our Lord whether these pure spirits remained constantly at the side of defiled sinners. Jesus answered, "Even if they do not always make their presence felt, yet they speak to their hearts from time to time, to bring them to a return. **Only at the judgment seat of God will the Angels entirely abandon the impenitent sinners.**"

At these words, Margaret reflected upon her former resistance to the admonitions of her Angel and wept bitterly. But Our Lord consoled her, saying that her former ingratitude was now forgotten and that her Angel now led her on the way of salvation, solving her doubts, defending her in temptations and strengthening her in afflictions.

## Chapter 6
# Visible "Guardian Angels"

Finally, there is a very particular admonition for each one of us contained in the office of the holy Guardian Angels, namely, that we should make it our holy duty to be, in imitation of them, visible guardian angels of others, counseling, helping and doing good to them. How often do we not have an opportunity to ward off evil and further the good of another! A single word at the right time, a single encouragement, a single reproof is often sufficient to preserve a soul from sin.

This office of angel guardian God has conferred especially upon you, **Christian parents**. In you the heavenly Guardians ought to find their most powerful and faithful allies. May the fidelity of the Angels serve as your model in fulfilling your holy task of rearing your children. May you, with angelic zeal, protect and watch over the **immortal souls** of those whom God has entrusted to your care and for whom you must one day render an account. Pray for your children to their holy Angels, and where your eye cannot accompany them, commend them especially to the care of their holy Guardians. Teach them at an early age to love and venerate their holy Guardian Angels. Implant in them a reverent remembrance of the presence of their Angel, that they may not do or say anything in his presence which they would not do or say in yours. Take care, above all, not to give them a bad example.

Be careful, too, to provide them with an education in which their Catholic Faith and morals will be fostered and protected. And when, in maturer years, they leave home to take up a profession or for other purposes, be sure that they are in good keeping.

## Chapter 7

# Devotions in Honor of Our Guardian Angels

## Mass of the Guardian Angels
### October 2

*Proper for October 2 from the Traditional Roman Rite.*

**Introit**. (*Ps.* 102:20). Bless the Lord, all ye his angels: you that are mighty in strength and execute his word, hearkening to the voice of his orders. *Ps.* Bless the Lord, O my soul: and let all that is within me bless his holy name. *V.* Glory be to the Father and to the Son and to the Holy Ghost, as it was in the beginning, is now, and ever shall be, world without end. Amen.

**Collect**. O God, Who in Thine unspeakable providence dost vouchsafe to send Thy holy Angels to keep watch over us, grant to us, Thy suppliants, that we may always be shielded by their protection and may rejoice in their fellowship forevermore. Through Our Lord Jesus Christ, Thy Son, who liveth and reigneth with Thee in the unity of the Holy Ghost, one God, world without end. Amen.

51

**Epistle**. (*Exod.* 23:20-23). Thus saith the Lord
God: Behold I will send my angel, who shall go
before thee and keep thee in thy journey and
bring thee into the place that I have prepared.
Take notice of him and hear his voice, and do not
think him one to be contemned, for he will not
forgive when thou hast sinned, and my name is in
him. But if thou wilt hear his voice and do all that
I speak, I will be an enemy to thy enemies and will
afflict them that afflict thee. And my angel shall go
before thee.

**Gradual**. (*Ps.* 90). God hath given his angels
charge over thee, to keep thee in all thy ways. *V.* In
their hands they shall bear thee up, lest at any
time thou dash thy foot against a stone. Alleluia,
alleluia. *V.* (*Ps.* 102:21). Bless the Lord, all ye his
hosts: you ministers of his that do his will. Alleluia.

**Gospel**. (*Matt.* 18:1-10). At that hour the disciples came to Jesus, saying: Who thinkest thou is
the greater in the kingdom of heaven? And Jesus
calling unto him a little child, set him in the midst
of them, and said: Amen I say to you, unless you
be converted and become as little children, you
shall not enter into the kingdom of heaven.
Whosoever therefore shall humble himself as this
little child, he is the greater in the kingdom of
heaven. And he that shall receive one such little
child in my name, receiveth me. But he that shall
scandalize one of these little ones that believe in
me, it were better for him that a millstone should
be hanged about his neck and that he should be

drowned in the depth of the sea. Woe to the world because of scandals. For it must needs be that scandals come: but nevertheless woe to that man by whom the scandal cometh. And if thy hand or thy foot scandalize thee, cut it off and cast it from thee. It is better for thee to go into life maimed or lame, than having two hands or two feet, to be cast into everlasting fire. And if thy eye scandalize thee, pluck it out and cast it from thee. It is better for thee having one eye to enter into life, than having two eyes to be cast into hell fire. See that you despise not one of these little ones, for I say to you that their angels in heaven always see the face of my Father who is in heaven.

**Offertory**. (*Ps.* 102:20-21). Bless the Lord, all ye his angels, you ministers of his that execute his word, hearkening to the voice of his orders.

**Secret**. Receive, O Lord, the gifts which we bring Thee in honor of Thy holy angels, and grant, in Thy mercy, that by their unceasing watchfulness we may be delivered from present dangers and may attain unto everlasting life. Through Our Lord Jesus Christ, Thy Son, who liveth and reigneth with Thee in the unity of the Holy Ghost, one God, world without end. Amen.

**Communion**. (*Dan.* 3:58). All ye angels of the Lord, bless the Lord: sing a hymn and exalt him above all forever.

**Postcommunion**. We have received, O Lord, Thy Divine mysteries, rejoicing in the festival of Thy holy angels; by their protection, we beseech

Thee, may we ever be delivered from the wiles of our enemies and guarded against all harm. Through Our Lord Jesus Christ, Thy Son, who liveth and reigneth with Thee in the unity of the Holy Ghost, one God, world without end. Amen.

## Litany of the Holy Guardian Angel

*(For private use only.)*

Lord, have mercy on us.
*Christ, have mercy on us.*
Lord, have mercy on us. Christ, hear us.
*Christ, graciously hear us.*
God the Father of Heaven,
*Have mercy on us.*
God the Son, Redeemer
of the world,
*Have mercy on us.*
God the Holy Ghost,
*Have mercy on us.*
Holy Trinity, One God,
*Have mercy on us.*

Holy Mary, Queen of the Angels, *pray for us.*
Holy Angel, my guardian, *pray for us.*
Holy Angel, my prince, *etc.*
Holy Angel, my monitor,

Holy Angel, my counselor,
Holy Angel, my defender,
Holy Angel, my steward,
Holy Angel, my friend,
Holy Angel, my negotiator,
Holy Angel, my intercessor,
Holy Angel, my patron,
Holy Angel, my director,
Holy Angel, my ruler,
Holy Angel, my protector,
Holy Angel, my comforter,
Holy Angel, my brother,
Holy Angel, my teacher,
Holy Angel, my shepherd,
Holy Angel, my witness,
Holy Angel, my helper,
Holy Angel, my watcher,
Holy Angel, my conductor,
Holy Angel, my preserver,
Holy Angel, my instructor,
Holy Angel, my enlightener,

Lamb of God, Who takest away the sins
   of the world,
   *Spare us, O Lord.*
Lamb of God, Who takest away the sins
   of the world,
   *Graciously hear us, O Lord.*
Lamb of God, Who takest away the sins
   of the world,
   *Have mercy on us.* *(Continued next page.)*

Christ, hear us.
  *Christ, graciously hear us.*
Lord, have mercy on us.

V.  Pray for us, O holy Guardian Angel,
R. *That we may be made worthy of the
    promises of Christ.*

### Let Us Pray

Almighty and everlasting God, Who in the counsel of Thine ineffable goodness hast appointed to all the Faithful, from their mother's womb, a special Angel Guardian of their body and soul, grant that I may so love and honor him whom Thou hast so mercifully given me that, protected by the bounty of Thy grace and by his assistance, I may merit to behold, with him and all the angelic hosts, the glory of Thy countenance in the heavenly kingdom, Thou Who livest and reignest world without end. R. *Amen.*

## Novena Prayer

*(A novena is made by praying a prayer
for nine days in succession.)*

O HOLY ANGEL, whom God, by the effect of His goodness and His tender regard for my welfare, has charged with the care of my conduct, and who assists me in all my wants and comforts me in all my afflictions, who supports me when I am discouraged and continually obtains for me new favors, I return thee profound thanks, and I earnestly beseech thee, O most amiable protector, to continue thy charitable care and defense of me against the malignant attacks of all my enemies. Keep me away from all occasions of sin. Obtain for me the grace of listening attentively to thy holy inspirations and of faithfully putting them into practice. In particular, I implore thee to obtain for me the favor which I ask for by this novena. *(Here mention your petition.)* Protect me in all the temptations and trials of this life, but more especially at the hour of my death, and do not leave me until thou hast conducted me into the presence of my Creator in the mansions of everlasting happiness. *Amen.*

## Prayer for a Happy Death
### *By St. Charles Borromeo*

IN THE NAME of the Most Holy Trinity, Father, Son and Holy Ghost, I, a poor, unhappy sinner, make this solemn declaration before thee, O beloved Angel, who has been given me as a protector by the Divine Majesty:

1. I desire to die in the Faith which the Holy, Roman and Apostolic Church adheres to and defends, in which all the Saints of the New Testa-

ment have died. I pray thee, provide that I may not depart out of this life before the Holy Sacraments of that Church have been administered to me.

2. I pray that I may depart from this life under thy holy protection and guidance, and I beseech thee, therefore, to assist me at the hour of my death and to propitiate the Eternal Judge, whose Sacred Heart was inflamed with most ardent love for sinners upon the Cross.

3. With my whole heart I long to be made a partaker of the merits of Jesus Christ and His holy Mother Mary, thine exalted Queen, and I pray thee, through the sufferings of Jesus on the Cross, to mitigate the agonies of my death and to move the Queen of Heaven to cast her loving glance upon me, a poor sinner, in that dreadful hour, for my sweetest consolation.

O my dearest Guardian Angel! Let my soul be placed in thy charge, and when it has gone forth from the prison of this body, do thou deliver it into the hands of its Creator and Redeemer, that with thee and all the Saints, it may gaze upon Him in the bliss of Heaven, love Him perfectly and find its blessedness in Him throughout eternity. Amen.

## Angel of God

ANGEL OF GOD, my Guardian dear,
To whom His love commits me here,
Ever this day *(or night)* be at my side,
To light and guard, to rule and guide. Amen.

## Prayer to Our Guardian Angel

O HOLY Guardian Angel, my dear friend and solicitous guide on the dangerous way of life, to thee be heartfelt thanks for the numberless benefits which have been granted me through thy love and goodness and for the powerful help by which thou hast preserved me from so many dangers and temptations. I beg of thee, let me further experience thy love and thy care. Avert from me all danger, increase in me horror for sin and love for all that is good. Be a counselor and consoler to me in all the affairs of my life, and when my life draws to a close, conduct my soul through the valley of death into the kingdom of eternal peace, so that in eternity we may together praise God and rejoice in His glory. Through Jesus Christ Our Lord. Amen.

O Angel of God, make me worthy of thy tender love, thy celestial companionship and thy never-failing protection!

## Good Night Prayer

G OOD NIGHT, my Guardian Angel,
   The day has sped away;
Well spent or ill, its story
Is written down for aye.

And now, of God's kind Providence,
Thou image pure and bright,
Watch o'er me while I'm sleeping—
My Angel dear, good night!

## Ejaculations

Hail, glorious Angel, appointed by God to be my guardian!

Hail, holy Angel, my protector in all dangers!

Hail, holy Angel, my defense in all afflictions!

Hail, holy Angel, my most faithful friend!

Hail, holy Angel, my guide!

Hail, holy Angel, my preceptor!

Hail, holy Angel, witness of all my actions!

Hail, holy Angel, my helper in every difficulty!

Hail, holy Angel, my counselor in doubt!

Hail, holy Angel, my shield at the hour of death!

## Prayer to All the Guardian Angels

O PURE AND HAPPY spirits whom the Almighty selected to become the Angels and Guardians of men, I most humbly prostrate myself before thee to thank thee for the charity and zeal with which thou dost execute this commission. Alas, how many pass a long life without ever thanking their invisible friends, to whom they owe a thousand times their preservation!

O charitable Guardians of those souls for whom Christ died, O flaming spirits who cannot avoid loving those whom Jesus eternally loved, permit me to address thee on behalf of all those committed to thy care, to implore for each of them a grateful sense of thy many favors and also the grace to profit by thy charitable assistance.

O Angels of those happy infants who as yet are "without spot before God," I earnestly beseech thee to preserve their innocence.

O Angels of youth, conduct them, exposed to so many dangers, safely to the bosom of God, as Tobias was conducted back to his father.

O Angels of those who employ themselves in the instruction of youth, animate them with thy zeal and love, teach them to emulate thy purity and continual view of God, that they may worthily and successfully co-operate with the invisible Guardians of their young charges.

O Angels of the clergy, of those "who have the

eternal Gospel to preach to them that sit upon the earth," present their words, their actions and their intentions to God, and purify them in that fire of love which consumes thee.

O Angels of the missionaries who have left their native land and all who were dear to them in order to preach the Gospel in foreign fields, protect them from the dangers which threaten them, especially from contact with ferocious animals and poisonous snakes; console them in their hours of depression and solitude, and lead them to those souls who are in danger of dying without Baptism.

O Angels of infidels and pagans, whom the True Faith has never enlightened, intercede for them, that they may open their hearts to the rays of grace, respond to the message delivered by God's missioners and acknowledge and adore the one true God.

O Angels of all who travel by air, land or water, be their guides and companions; protect them from all dangers of collision, fire and explosion and lead them safely to their destination.

O Guardian Angels of sinners, charitable guides of those unhappy mortals whose perseverance in sin would embitter even thine unutterable joys, wert thou not established in the peace of God; oh, join me, I ardently beseech thee, in imploring their conversion!

And thou, O Guardian Angels of the sick, I entreat thee especially to help, console and implore the spirit of joy for all those who are deprived of health, which is among God's most precious gifts to man. Intercede for them, that they may not succumb to despondency or lose by impatience the merits they can gain in carrying with resignation and joy the cross which Christ has laid upon them as a special token of His love.

O Angels of those who at this moment struggle in the agonies of death, strengthen, encourage and defend them against the attacks of their infernal enemy.

O faithful guides, holy spirits, adorers of the Divinity, Guardian Angels of all creatures, protect us all; teach us to love, to pray, to wage combat on earth, so that one day we may reach Heaven and there be happy for all eternity! Amen.


## Prayer to Our Guardian Angel
*By St. Gertrude*

O MOST HOLY ANGEL of God, appointed by Him to be my guardian, I give thee thanks for all the benefits which thou hast ever bestowed on me in body and in soul. I praise and glorify thee that thou dost condescend to assist me with such patient fidelity and to defend me against all the assaults of my enemies. Blessed be the hour in which thou wast assigned to me for my guardian, my defender and my patron. In acknowledgment of and in return for all thy loving ministries to me from my youth up, I offer thee the infinitely precious and noble Heart of Jesus, and I firmly purpose to obey thee henceforward and most faithfully to serve my God. Amen.

*If you have enjoyed this book, consider making your next selection from among the following . . .*

Prices subject to change.

Prices subject to change.